1.

-- 1

Summary 3

Chapter 2 6

Chapter 1: Introduction to YouTube for Adults 9

Chapter 2: Identifying Your Niche 17

Chapter 3: Content Creation Strategies 26

Chapter 4: Time Management for Content Creators .. 35

Chapter 5: Mastering SEO Optimization 44

Chapter 6: Monetization Strategies 53

Chapter 7: Building a Community on YouTube 61

Chapter 8: Navigating Challenges as an Adult YouTuber 70

Chapter 9: Advanced Video Production Techniques . 79

Chapter 10: Social Media Integration and Cross-Promotion 87

Chapter 11: Analytics and Performance Tracking 96

Chapter 12: Future Trends in Digital Content Creation 105

Synopsis..114

    2.

    3.

    4.

    5.

    6.

    7.

    8.

    9.

    10.

    11.

    12.

    13.

    14.

    15.

    16.

Summary

Chapter 1: Introduction to YouTube for Adults   3

1.1 Understanding the Digital Landscape   3

1.2 Overcoming Common Misconceptions   5

1.3 The Importance of Niche Selection   7

Chapter 2: Identifying Your Niche   9

2.1 Exercises for Refining Your Focus   9

2.2 Research Methods for Validating Your Niche   11

2.3 Case Studies: Successful Adult YouTubers   13

Chapter 3: Content Creation Strategies   15

3.1 Planning and Scripting Engaging Videos   15

3.2 Filming Techniques for High-Quality Production   17

3.3 Editing Tips for Busy Adults

19

Chapter 4: Time Management for Content Creators

21

4.1 Balancing YouTube with Full-Time Work and Family

21

4.2 Efficient Content Creation Schedules

23

4.3 Automating and Outsourcing Tasks

25

Chapter 5: Mastering SEO Optimization

27

5.1 Keywords, Tags, and Descriptions

27

5.2 Understanding YouTube's Algorithm

29

5.3 Tools and Resources for SEO Success

31

Chapter 6: Monetization Strategies

33

6.1 Exploring Ad Revenue Opportunities

33

6.2 Diversifying Income through Sponsorships and Merchandise   35

6.3 Leveraging Membership Platforms   37

Chapter 7: Building a Community on YouTube
39

7.1 Engaging with Your Audience Effectively
39

7.2 Encouraging Viewer Loyalty
41

7.3 Managing Comments and Feedback
43

Chapter 8: Navigating Challenges as an Adult YouTuber
45

8.1 Dealing with Criticism and Negative Comments
45

8.2 Managing Privacy Concerns Online
47

8.3 Staying Motivated During Slow Growth Periods
49

Chapter 9: Advanced Video Production Techniques
51

9.1 Lighting and Sound Optimization
51

9.2 Advanced Editing Skills
53

9.3 Creating a Consistent Brand Aesthetic

Chapter 10: Social Media Integration and Cross-Promotion 55

10.1 Utilizing Social Media to Boost Visibility 57

10.2 Collaborations with Other Creators 57

10.3 Effective Cross-Promotion Strategies 59

Chapter 11: Analytics and Performance Tracking 61

11.1 Setting Up YouTube Analytics 63

11.2 Interpreting Data to Guide Strategy 63

11.3 Adjusting Content Based on Performance Insights 65

Chapter 12: Future Trends in Digital Content Creation 67

12.1 Emerging Technologies Impacting YouTube 69

12.2 Adapting to Changes in Viewer Behavior 69

12.3 Planning for Long-Term Growth on the Platform 71

73

1

Introduction to YouTube for Adults

1.1 Understanding the Digital Landscape

The digital landscape, particularly within the realm of YouTube, presents a unique set of opportunities and challenges for adults looking to establish their presence. This platform has evolved into a vast ecosystem where content is not just consumed passively but also engages viewers in meaningful ways. For adults venturing into this space, understanding this digital terrain is crucial for navigating it effectively and leveraging its potential to the fullest.

At its core, YouTube thrives on diversity and authenticity, making it an ideal platform for adults with rich life experiences and unique perspectives to share. However, the sheer volume of content and creators can make standing out a significant challenge. This necessitates a deep dive into strategic planning, niche identification, and audience understanding. Adults entering YouTube must recognize that success on this platform goes beyond mere content creation; it involves building a brand that resonates with viewers on a personal level.

In conclusion, mastering the digital landscape of YouTube requires more than just creativity; it demands resilience, adaptability, and continuous learning. For adults ready to embark on this journey, recognizing the importance of strategic planning, audience engagement, and personal branding will be key determinants of success in carving out their niche within this dynamic platform.

- Navigating Algorithm Changes: YouTube's algorithm is notoriously complex and ever-changing. Adults need to stay informed about these changes to ensure their content remains visible and relevant. This includes understanding how factors like watch time, viewer engagement, and video metadata influence content discovery.

- Understanding Audience Demographics: Identifying and understanding one's target audience is critical. Adults should leverage analytics tools provided by YouTube to gain insights into who their viewers are, what they prefer watching, and when they are most active online.

- Balancing Responsibilities: Many adults face the challenge of balancing content creation with other responsibilities such as full-time employment or family commitments. Effective time management strategies become indispensable in this context.

1.2 Overcoming Common Misconceptions

Entering the world of YouTube can often be met with preconceived notions that may deter or mislead adults from fully embracing and leveraging this platform. A critical step in navigating YouTube successfully involves debunking these myths and understanding the reality of content creation and audience engagement.

One prevalent misconception is that YouTube is primarily for younger audiences and creators. This belief can make adults feel out of place or irrelevant on the platform. However, YouTube's audience is incredibly diverse, spanning various age groups, interests, and demographics. Adults bring a wealth of experience and perspective that can appeal to viewers seeking content beyond the realms typically associated with younger creators.

Another common myth is that success on YouTube requires viral hits or sensational content. While viral videos can indeed catapult a creator to fame, sustainable growth on YouTube is built on consistency, authenticity, and engagement with one's community. Many successful channels focus on niche topics, providing value through expertise or unique viewpoints rather than chasing trends.

- The Myth of Instant Success: Some adults may enter YouTube expecting immediate results in terms of subscribers and views. The reality is that building a channel takes time, patience, and perseverance. Success often comes from learning through trial and error, refining content strategies based on viewer feedback, and gradually growing an engaged audience.
- Misunderstanding Monetization: There's also a misconception about how monetization works on

YouTube. It's not solely about the number of views; factors such as audience retention, watch time, and engagement play significant roles in revenue generation. Understanding these nuances is crucial for adults aiming to monetize their content effectively.

- Overestimating Technical Requirements: Finally, some adults might be intimidated by perceived technical barriers to entry. While high-quality production can enhance videos, many successful YouTubers started with basic equipment. Content quality and authenticity often outweigh production value in terms of importance to viewers.

In conclusion, overcoming these common misconceptions requires a blend of realistic expectations, strategic planning, and a willingness to learn and adapt. By dispelling these myths, adults can approach YouTube with confidence and clarity, ready to carve out their space in its expansive digital landscape.

1.3 The Importance of Niche Selection

Selecting a niche is a pivotal step for adults entering the YouTube arena, acting as the foundation upon which a successful channel can be built. This process involves identifying a specific topic or area of interest that not only resonates with the creator but also addresses the needs and interests of a particular audience segment. The significance of niche selection cannot be overstated, as it directly influences content relevance, viewer engagement, and long-term channel growth.

Choosing the right niche allows creators to tailor their content to an audience that seeks expertise or entertainment in specific areas, ranging from educational tutorials to lifestyle vlogging. This focused approach helps in establishing a strong connection with viewers, fostering a sense of community around shared interests. Moreover, niches enable creators to differentiate themselves in a crowded marketplace by offering unique perspectives or specialized knowledge not readily available elsewhere on the platform.

Another critical aspect of niche selection is its impact on discoverability and monetization. YouTube's algorithm favors channels that consistently produce content within a particular niche, improving visibility among interested viewers. This targeted visibility is crucial for attracting subscribers who are more likely to engage with the content regularly, thereby enhancing watch time and other metrics important for monetization through YouTube's Partner Program.

- Alignment with Personal Passion: Selecting a niche aligned with one's interests ensures sustained motivation and authenticity, qualities highly valued by viewers.

- Expertise and Authority: Focusing on a specific area allows creators to establish themselves as authorities or go-to sources within their chosen field.

- Community Building: A well-defined niche fosters the development of an engaged community centered around mutual interests, leading to higher levels of interaction and loyalty.

In conclusion, niche selection is more than just an initial step in launching a YouTube channel; it's an ongoing strategy that shapes content creation, audience engagement, and overall channel identity. By carefully choosing and refining their niche, adult creators can carve out their own space on YouTube where they can share their passions, expertise, and unique perspectives with an appreciative audience.

References:

- YouTube Creator Academy. "Find Your Niche." An extensive guide that helps creators identify their unique selling points and target audience to build a successful YouTube channel.

- Derral Eves. "The YouTube Formula: How Anyone Can Unlock the Algorithm to Drive Views, Build an Audience, and Grow Revenue." This book provides insights into leveraging YouTube's algorithm by focusing on niche content creation.

- Roberto Blake. "Creating Awesome Content for YouTube." A video series that emphasizes the importance of niche selection in creating engaging and targeted content for viewers.

- Tim Schmoyer. "30 Days to a Better YouTube Channel." A course designed to improve channel performance through better understanding of audience needs and niche refinement.

2

Identifying Your Niche

2.1 Exercises for Refining Your Focus

Finding and refining your niche on YouTube is a critical step towards building a successful channel, especially for adults who are navigating the complexities of content creation alongside other responsibilities. This process involves deep introspection and strategic planning to ensure that your chosen niche not only aligns with your passions and expertise but also meets the needs and interests of a specific audience segment on YouTube.

To aid in this crucial phase, several exercises can be employed to sharpen your focus and carve out a unique space within the YouTube ecosystem. These exercises are designed not just to identify what you love talking about or creating content around, but also to pinpoint where those interests intersect with what viewers are seeking.

The culmination of these exercises should provide a clearer picture of where your passions align with market demand on YouTube. It's important to remember that refining your focus may require revisiting these steps multiple times as you grow and evolve on the platform. The goal is not just to find a niche but to continuously adapt and thrive within it amidst changing trends and audience preferences.

In conclusion, identifying and refining one's focus on YouTube demands both creativity and strategic thinking. By systematically working through these exercises, aspiring YouTubers can lay a solid foundation for their channel that resonates with both their personal aspirations and the broader community they aim to serve.

- Interest Inventory: Begin by listing all topics you are passionate about or have considerable knowledge in. Don't limit yourself—include everything from professional expertise to hobbies or even challenges you've overcome.

- Audience Pain Points: For each interest listed, research potential audience pain points or questions related to the topic. Utilize tools like Google Trends, YouTube search autocomplete, and forums relevant to your interests to understand what people are searching for.

- Competitive Analysis: Conduct a thorough analysis of existing channels within your areas of interest. Note what they do well and opportunities they might be missing, which could serve as an entry point for your unique angle on the subject matter.

- Content Differentiation Strategy: Based on your findings from the competitive analysis, develop a strategy that highlights how your content will differ. Consider aspects such as presentation style, depth of information, or innovative formats that could set your channel apart.

- Niche Validation Test: Before fully committing to a niche, test its viability by creating pilot content. Analyze viewer engagement through comments, likes/dislikes ratio, and view count to gauge whether there's genuine interest in more content within this niche.

2.2 Research Methods for Validating Your Niche

After refining your focus through introspection and strategic planning, the next crucial step is validating your niche. This phase involves employing various research methods to ensure that there is a demand for your content and that it has the potential to thrive on YouTube. Validation not only confirms the viability of your chosen niche but also minimizes the risk of investing time and resources into a market with limited growth potential.

To begin with, **keyword research** plays an essential role in niche validation. Tools like Google Keyword Planner and SEMrush can provide insights into search volumes, competition levels, and trending topics within your niche. By identifying keywords that have high search volumes but low competition, you can uncover gaps in the market that your channel could fill.

Social listening is another powerful method for validating your niche. Monitoring conversations on social media platforms, forums like Reddit, and Q&A sites such as Quora can help you understand what people are talking about in relation to your niche. This real-time feedback can reveal audience pain points, emerging trends, and frequently asked questions that your content could address.

- Analyzing competitor channels closely can offer valuable insights into what works well in your niche and where there might be opportunities for differentiation. Pay attention to their most popular videos, viewer engagement metrics (like comments and likes), and how they interact with their audience.

- Conducting surveys or interviews with potential viewers can provide direct feedback on their interests, preferences, and content consumption habits. This firsthand information is invaluable for tailoring your content strategy to meet audience needs effectively.

- Pilot testing with a small batch of content before fully committing to a niche allows you to gauge viewer response in a practical setting. Analyzing engagement metrics from these initial videos will help you determine if there's enough interest to sustain a channel focused on this topic.

In conclusion, validating your niche through comprehensive research is critical for building a successful YouTube channel. By combining keyword research, social listening, competitive analysis, direct audience feedback, and pilot testing, you can confidently proceed with creating content that resonates with viewers and fills an unmet need within the YouTube ecosystem.

2.3 Case Studies: Successful Adult YouTubers

The journey to becoming a successful YouTuber is as diverse as the platform's vast array of content. For adult YouTubers, who target an older demographic with more specialized interests, carving out a niche and validating it through strategic research is paramount. This section delves into the stories of several adult YouTubers who have not only identified their unique space within YouTube but have also thrived by engaging deeply with their audience and consistently delivering value.

One notable example is the channel "Financial Education," which simplifies complex financial concepts for everyday adults looking to improve their financial literacy. The creator behind this channel validated his niche through keyword research, identifying a high demand for financial advice paired with a lack of accessible, easy-to-understand content.

By focusing on trending topics within finance and responding to viewer feedback, he has built a loyal following that values his clear explanations and practical advice.

Another success story comes from "Yoga With Adriene," a channel that offers free yoga videos for all levels. Recognizing the growing interest in wellness and self-care, Adriene Mishler differentiated her content by emphasizing connection and mindfulness, appealing to adults seeking a personal touch in their fitness routines. Social listening played a crucial role in shaping her content strategy, allowing her to tap into the desires of her audience for yoga practices that catered to specific needs and moods.

- Analyzing competitors helped these creators identify gaps in the market where they could offer something unique or improve upon existing content.
- Direct feedback from viewers through comments and social media interactions provided insights into what content resonated most, guiding future video topics.

- Pilot testing new formats or series allowed them to experiment with innovative ideas while gauging audience interest before fully committing resources.

In conclusion, these case studies underscore the importance of thorough niche validation for adult YouTubers. By employing a combination of keyword research, social listening, competitive analysis, direct audience engagement, and pilot testing, they were able to create compelling content that not only filled an unmet need but also fostered strong community ties. Their success stories serve as inspiration for aspiring creators looking to make their mark on YouTube by addressing the specific interests and challenges of an adult audience.

References:

- "Financial Education YouTube Channel: Simplifying Finance for Adults." Accessed September 23, 2023. A case study on how the Financial Education channel has grown by making complex financial concepts accessible to adults.

- "Yoga With Adriene: Connecting Mindfulness and Fitness." Accessed September 23, 2023. An exploration of how Adriene Mishler's approach to yoga has cultivated a massive following by focusing on wellness and self-care.

- "The Role of Keyword Research in Successful YouTube Channels." Accessed September 23, 2023. This article discusses the importance of keyword research in identifying niche markets and content strategies for YouTubers.

- "Engaging with Your Audience: Lessons from Top YouTubers." Accessed September 23, 2023. Insights into how direct feedback and social media interactions can shape content creation and build viewer loyalty.

3

Content Creation Strategies

3.1 Planning and Scripting Engaging Videos

At the heart of successful YouTube content lies meticulous planning and scripting, especially for adults venturing into this dynamic platform. This phase is crucial as it sets the foundation for creating videos that not only captivate but also retain viewer interest. Planning involves identifying the core message of your video, understanding your target audience, and outlining the structure of your content. Scripting, on the other hand, translates these ideas into a coherent narrative, ensuring that every second of your video is engaging.

One key aspect of planning is setting clear objectives for each video. Whether it's to educate, entertain, or inspire, having a defined goal helps in crafting content that resonates with viewers. It's also essential to conduct thorough research on topics that interest your target demographic. This could involve analyzing trends within your niche or addressing common questions and challenges faced by your audience.

- Identifying Your Video's Objective: Start by defining what you want to achieve with each video.
- Audience Research: Dive deep into understanding who your viewers are and what they seek from your content.
- Content Structuring: Outline the main points you wish to cover in a logical sequence to keep viewers engaged.

Scripting transforms these elements into a detailed blueprint for your video. A well-crafted script guides not just what you say but how you say it, incorporating elements like storytelling and humor where appropriate. It should also include cues for visuals or b-roll footage to complement the narration, enhancing the overall viewing experience.

- Writing an Engaging Script: Focus on clarity and conciseness while weaving in storytelling elements to make your content relatable.

- Incorporating Visual Cues: Plan for visual elements that can support or enhance your narrative.

- Pacing Your Content: Ensure that your script allows for natural pauses and emphasizes key points effectively to maintain viewer interest throughout.

In conclusion, planning and scripting are indispensable steps in creating engaging YouTube videos. They require thoughtful consideration of one's objectives, audience insights, and creative execution strategies. By dedicating time to these initial stages, creators can significantly improve their chances of producing content that not only reaches but profoundly impacts their intended audience.

3.2 Filming Techniques for High-Quality Production

Filming techniques play a pivotal role in elevating the quality of video production, transforming basic content into cinematic experiences that captivate and engage audiences. This section delves into advanced filming strategies that can significantly enhance the visual appeal and effectiveness of your videos, ensuring they stand out in a crowded digital landscape.

Understanding the importance of camera angles and movement is fundamental. Each angle tells a different story and evokes distinct emotions, making it crucial to select the right perspective for each scene. For instance, low-angle shots can make subjects appear dominant or heroic, while high-angle shots often convey vulnerability or insignificance. Incorporating dynamic movements like pans, tilts, and dolly shots adds life to your videos, creating a more immersive viewing experience.

- Mastering Camera Angles: Experiment with various angles to discover how they impact narrative tone.
- Dynamic Movement: Use camera movements to add energy and depth to your scenes.
- Lighting Techniques: Harness natural and artificial light to set mood and focus attention.

Lighting is another critical element that can dramatically affect the quality of your footage. Proper lighting techniques help define the texture, depth, and atmosphere of your scenes. Whether utilizing natural light or investing in professional lighting equipment, understanding how to manipulate light will allow you to achieve the desired mood and aesthetic for your videos.

Finally, post-production plays an essential role in achieving high-quality production values. Editing not only involves cutting and assembling footage but also color grading, sound design, and adding visual effects that enhance storytelling. Color grading can alter the tone and mood of your video, while effective sound design can elevate the viewer's emotional response. Visual effects, when used judaniciouslylycan add polish and intrigue to your content.

- Editing for Cohesion: Trim footage strategically to maintain pacing and interest.
- Color Grading: Use color correction tools to enhance or alter the visual tone.
- Sound Design: Incorporate music, sound effects, and ambient sounds for a fuller sensory experience.

In conclusion, employing advanced filming techniques is crucial for creators aiming for high-quality video production. By mastering camera work, lighting setups, and post-production processes, you can produce content that not only looks professional but also deeply resonates with your audience. Remember that creativity combined with technical skill will set your videos apart in today's competitive content landscape.

3.3 Editing Tips for Busy Adults

In today's fast-paced world, busy adults often find themselves juggling multiple responsibilities alongside their passion for content creation. Editing, a crucial step in the production process, can be particularly time-consuming and daunting for those with limited hours in their day. This section aims to provide practical editing tips tailored for busy adults, enabling them to produce high-quality content efficiently.

Firstly, understanding the power of efficient workflow is essential. Establishing a streamlined editing process saves precious time and energy. Begin by organizing your footage and assets before you start editing. Labeling clips and using folders will help you navigate your files quickly, reducing the time spent searching for specific shots or audio files.

- Pre-Editing Organization: Spend time upfront to categorize and label your files.

- Keyboard Shortcuts Mastery: Learn and utilize keyboard shortcuts for your editing software to significantly speed up the editing process.

- Template Use: Create or use existing templates for recurring projects to minimize repetitive work.

Another vital strategy is leveraging technology to automate repetitive tasks. Many modern editing software options offer features like auto-syncing audio and video or automatic color correction. Taking advantage of these tools can dramatically reduce manual labor, allowing you to focus on creative aspects of editing that require a human touch.

Beyond technical efficiencies, adopting a minimalist approach to editing can also be beneficial. Resist the urge to over-edit; simplicity often leads to more powerful storytelling. Focus on cutting out unnecessary parts of your footage and keeping transitions clean and straightforward. This not only speeds up the editing process but also results in a more engaging final product for your audience.

- Selective Editing: Be ruthless in cutting unnecessary content to maintain pacing and interest.
- Batch Processing: Group similar tasks together (e.g., color correction) to streamline your workflow.
- Feedback Loops: Share early edits with trusted peers or mentors to identify areas for improvement efficiently.

In conclusion, by implementing these strategies—organizing files effectively, mastering software shortcuts, utilizing templates, automating repetitive tasks, adopting a minimalist approach, batch processing tasks, and seeking early feedback—busy adults can optimize their editing process. These practices not only save time but also enhance the quality of content produced, ensuring that even the busiest creators can achieve their creative visions without sacrificing other life commitments.

References:

- Adobe Creative Cloud Team. "The Ultimate Guide to Video Editing."
- Frame.io Team. "10 Tips for Faster Editing in Any Software."

- PremiumBeat by Shutterstock. "5 Essential Tips for Organizing Your Video Editing Projects."
- No Film School. "Tips for Faster Editing."

4

Time Management for Content Creators

4.1 Balancing YouTube with Full-Time Work and Family

For many aspiring YouTubers, the dream of channel growth often clashes with the reality of daily responsibilities. Adults juggling full-time jobs and family commitments may find the prospect of creating content overwhelming. However, with strategic planning and efficient management, it is possible to cultivate a successful YouTube presence without sacrificing personal or professional obligations.

The first step in this balancing act is to establish a realistic content creation schedule. This involves assessing one's weekly commitments and identifying potential time slots dedicated to filming, editing, and engaging with your audience. It might mean waking up an hour earlier or utilizing weekends effectively. The key is consistency; even if you can only commit to producing one video per week, maintaining a regular posting schedule is crucial for audience retention.

- Prioritize tasks: Not all content creation activities require the same level of effort and time. Identify high-impact tasks that contribute most significantly to your channel's growth and prioritize them.

- Batch content creation: Dedicate specific days to filming multiple videos or segments thereof. This approach not only saves time but also reduces the frequency of setting up recording equipment.

- Leverage technology: Utilize tools and software that streamline the editing process or automate certain aspects of content management, such as scheduling posts or analyzing viewer engagement.

Incorporating family into your YouTube journey can also serve as a unique way to balance personal life with content creation. Whether it's featuring family members in videos where appropriate or involving them in brainstorming sessions for new content ideas, integrating these two aspects of your life can create authentic and relatable content that resonates with viewers who share similar life stages.

Finally, setting clear boundaries between work, family time, and YouTube endeavors is essential. Communicate openly with loved ones about your goals and the importance of designated recording times. Establishing these boundaries ensures that while you are building your digital presence, you are not compromising on quality time with family or neglecting professional responsibilities.

Balancing YouTube aspirations with full-time work and family requires thoughtful planning, discipline, and creativity. By adopting these strategies, adults can navigate their multifaceted roles successfully while pursuing their passion for content creation on one of the world's largest platforms.

4.2 Efficient Content Creation Schedules

Creating an efficient content creation schedule is pivotal for YouTubers who are striving to balance their passion with personal and professional responsibilities. This section delves into strategies that enable content creators to maximize productivity without compromising the quality of their output or their well-being. An effective schedule not only helps in maintaining a consistent posting rhythm but also ensures that creators can sustain their enthusiasm for content creation over the long term.

To begin, it's essential to conduct a thorough self-assessment of one's daily routines and obligations. Identifying blocks of time that can be consistently dedicated to content creation each week is the foundation of an efficient schedule. This might involve early mornings, late evenings, or segments of weekends, depending on individual circumstances and energy levels.

- Set Realistic Goals: Understand your capacity and set achievable goals regarding how many videos you can produce within a given timeframe. Overcommitting can lead to burnout and affect the quality of your content.

- Theme Days: Allocate specific days for different aspects of content creation - such as research, filming, editing, and community engagement. This approach allows for deep focus on one task at a time, making the process more manageable and less overwhelming.

- Time Blocking: Use time blocking techniques to dedicate uninterrupted periods to content creation tasks. This method helps in minimizing distractions and increasing productivity during designated work times.

Incorporating flexibility into your schedule is also crucial. Life's unpredictability means that rigid schedules often fall apart under pressure. Allowing some leeway in your planning accommodates unexpected events or shifts in priorities without derailing your entire content production process.

Moreover, leveraging technology can significantly enhance scheduling efficiency. Various apps and tools are available that assist in task management, automating social media posts, and tracking progress towards goals. Embracing these resources can free up valuable time that can be redirected towards creative endeavors or rest.

In conclusion, crafting an efficient content creation schedule requires a blend of realistic goal-setting, strategic planning, disciplined execution, and adaptability to change. By adopting these practices, YouTubers can navigate the challenges of balancing content creation with other life commitments more effectively, leading to sustained growth and fulfillment in their creative pursuits.

4.3 Automating and Outsourcing Tasks

In the realm of content creation, time is a precious commodity that seems to be in perpetual short supply. As creators strive to maintain a balance between producing high-quality content and managing the myriad other responsibilities that life throws their way, automating and outsourcing emerge as invaluable strategies for maximizing efficiency and productivity. This section delves into how these approaches can significantly alleviate the workload on creators, allowing them to focus more on their creative endeavors.

Automation refers to the use of technology to perform tasks without human intervention. In the context of content creation, this can range from scheduling social media posts in advance using tools like Buffer or Hootsuite, to employing software that automates video editing processes or streamlines email responses. Automation not only saves time but also ensures consistency in engagement with audiences, an essential factor in building and maintaining a strong online presence.

- Social Media Management: Automating posts across various platforms can help maintain a consistent posting schedule, crucial for audience retention and growth.

- Email Marketing: Tools like Mailchimp automate email campaigns, enabling creators to efficiently communicate with their subscribers while focusing on content production.

- Content Planning: Utilizing project management tools such as Trello or Asana for planning and tracking content production stages streamlines workflow and enhances productivity.

Outsourcing involves delegating certain tasks or projects to external parties or freelancers. This strategy is particularly beneficial for tasks that require specialized skills or for aspects of content creation that are time-consuming. For instance, hiring a freelance editor to refine videos can drastically reduce turnaround times while ensuring professional quality. Similarly, engaging graphic designers for thumbnails or website design can elevate the aesthetic appeal of one's digital presence without detracting from the time available for content ideation and creation.

- Video Editing: Outsourcing editing can save countless hours while ensuring your videos have a professional touch.
- Graphic Design: Professional designers can create visually appealing thumbnails, logos, and channel art that stand out.
- Content Writing: Hiring writers for blog posts or scripts can enhance quality and consistency across different types of content.

In conclusion, effectively leveraging automation and outsourcing not only optimizes time management but also plays a critical role in scaling content production without compromising quality. By embracing these strategies, creators can allocate more time towards innovation and creativity—core components that fuel growth in the competitive landscape of digital content creation.

References:

- Buffer. (n.d.). Social Media Management Platform. Retrieved from https://buffer.com

- Hootsuite. (n.d.). Manage Your Social Media in One Place. Retrieved from https://hootsuite.com

- Mailchimp. (n.d.). Marketing, Automation & Email Platform. Retrieved from https://mailchimp.com

- Trello. (n.d.). Collaborate On Projects From Beginning To End. Retrieved from https://trello.com

- Asana. (n.d.). Work Management Platform. Retrieved from https://asana.com

5

Mastering SEO Optimization

5.1 Keywords, Tags, and Descriptions

The digital landscape is fiercely competitive, especially for content creators aiming to establish a presence on platforms like YouTube. For adults venturing into this realm, understanding the power of keywords, tags, and descriptions can significantly enhance their visibility and engagement rates. This section delves into how these elements work in synergy to optimize search engine results and why they are crucial for anyone looking to grow their channel.

Keywords are the cornerstone of SEO optimization. They are not just words; they are reflections of what potential viewers are searching for. Identifying the right keywords requires research and understanding of one's niche. Tools like Google Keyword Planner or YouTube's Search Suggest feature can offer insights into popular search terms related to your content. Incorporating these keywords naturally into your video titles, descriptions, and even within your content itself can dramatically improve your visibility on YouTube.

Tags serve as additional metadata that help categorize your videos more effectively. While viewers may not see these tags, YouTube's algorithm uses them to understand the context of your videos and suggest them in relevant searches. It's important to use a mix of broad and specific tags to cover various search intents.

- Use primary keywords as your first few tags.
- Include variations of your main keyword to cover common search queries.
- Add category-specific tags to help YouTube understand where your video fits.

Descriptions provide a broader canvas to utilize keywords and convey what your video is about. A well-crafted description with strategically placed keywords can make your video more discoverable. However, it's essential to write for humans first—ensuring readability and engagement—while subtly integrating SEO practices.

- Start with a compelling summary that includes primary keywords within the first two sentences.
- Incorporate secondary keywords naturally throughout the text.
- Add links to social media profiles or websites to encourage further engagement outside YouTube.

In conclusion, mastering the art of using keywords, tags, and descriptions is fundamental for any adult looking to grow on YouTube. By carefully researching and implementing these elements in harmony with each other, creators can significantly increase their chances of being discovered by their target audience. Remember, consistency in applying these techniques across all videos will compound over time, leading to sustained growth and success on the platform.

5.2 Understanding YouTube's Algorithm

Grasping the intricacies of YouTube's algorithm is pivotal for anyone looking to make an impact on this vast platform. Unlike simple keyword, tag, and description optimization, understanding the algorithm requires a deeper dive into how YouTube evaluates and prioritizes content for its users. This exploration goes beyond basic SEO techniques, delving into the mechanics of viewer engagement and content visibility.

YouTube's algorithm has evolved significantly since its inception, with a current focus on user engagement and satisfaction. This includes metrics such as watch time, viewer retention, and interaction rate (likes, comments, shares). Videos that perform well on these fronts are more likely to be recommended by YouTube to a broader audience. Therefore, creating content that not only attracts viewers but also keeps them engaged throughout is crucial.

- Watch Time: The total duration a viewer spends watching your video. Longer watch times signal to YouTube that your content is engaging and worth recommending.

- Viewer Retention: This metric indicates what percentage of your video is watched by viewers. High retention rates suggest that your content is compelling and relevant from start to finish.

- Interaction Rate: Likes, comments, shares, and even the number of new subscribers after watching a video contribute to its interaction rate. A high interaction rate demonstrates active viewer engagement with your content.

To optimize for YouTube's algorithm, creators must focus on producing high-quality videos that engage viewers right from the beginning. Strategies include using captivating thumbnails and titles to attract clicks and designing video intros that hook viewers immediately. Additionally, encouraging viewer interaction by asking questions or prompting discussions in the comments can further enhance engagement metrics.

In conclusion, while keywords, tags, and descriptions lay the foundation for SEO optimization on YouTube, mastering the platform's algorithm demands an understanding of complex viewer engagement metrics. By focusing on creating engaging content that resonates with their audience, creators can significantly improve their visibility on YouTube. Remembering that at its core, YouTube aims to keep users on the platform longer by suggesting videos they are likely to enjoy underscores the importance of aligning content creation strategies with these goals.

5.3 Tools and Resources for SEO Success

The landscape of Search Engine Optimization (SEO) is ever-evolving, with new strategies and technologies emerging regularly. To stay ahead in this dynamic field, leveraging the right tools and resources is crucial. These instruments not only simplify the complex process of SEO but also provide insights that can significantly enhance the visibility and ranking of your content on search engines.

Understanding the vast array of tools available can be overwhelming, yet selecting the appropriate ones is essential for effective SEO management. From keyword research to performance analytics, each tool serves a specific purpose in the optimization process.

- Keyword Research Tools: Platforms like Google Keyword Planner, SEMrush, and Ahrefs are invaluable for identifying high-value keywords. They offer insights into search volume, competition level, and keyword relevance, enabling you to craft content that aligns with what your audience is searching for.

- Content Optimization Tools: Tools such as Yoast SEO and Clearscope assist in optimizing content around selected keywords. They provide suggestions on readability, keyword density, and other elements that influence how well your content ranks.

- Technical SEO Auditors: Websites need to be technically sound to rank well. Screaming Frog SEO Spider and Google's PageSpeed Insights analyze your website's technical health, identifying issues like broken links, slow loading times, and crawl errors that could negatively impact your SEO.

- Analytics and Performance Tracking: Understanding how your content performs is key to refining your SEO strategy. Google Analytics and Google Search Console offer comprehensive insights into website traffic patterns, user behavior, and performance in search results. This data allows you to adjust tactics for better outcomes.

    Beyond individual tools, staying informed through reputable SEO blogs and forums such as Moz Blog, Search Engine Journal, or Webmaster World is equally important. These platforms share updates on algorithm changes, new optimization techniques, and case studies from industry experts.

In conclusion, mastering SEO requires more than just understanding its principles; it demands the strategic use of specialized tools and resources. By integrating these into your optimization efforts—coupled with continuous learning—you can significantly improve your online presence and achieve long-term success in search engine rankings.

References:

- Google Keyword Planner: https://ads.google.com/home/tools/keyword-planner/
- SEMrush: https://www.semrush.com/
- Ahrefs: https://ahrefs.com/
- Yoast SEO: https://yoast.com/
- Clearscope: https://www.clearscope.io/
- Screaming Frog SEO Spider: https://www.screamingfrog.co.uk/seo-spider/
- Google's PageSpeed Insights: https://developers.google.com/speed/pagespeed/insights/

- Google Analytics: htttps://analytics.google.com/analytics/web/

- Google Search Console: https://search.google.com/search-console/about

- Moz Blog: htttps://moz.com/blog

- Search Engine Journal: htttps://www.searchenginejournal.com/

- Webmaster World: http:/webmasterworld./com/a>/l/i></ul>i

6

Monetization Strategies

6.1 Exploring Ad Revenue Opportunities

The digital landscape offers a plethora of ad revenue opportunities for content creators, especially on platforms like YouTube. Understanding and leveraging these opportunities can significantly contribute to a channel's financial success. This exploration delves into the various facets of ad revenue generation, providing insights beyond the basics covered in initial summaries.

At its core, ad revenue on YouTube is primarily generated through the YouTube Partner Program (YPP), which allows creators to earn money from ads displayed on their videos. However, maximizing this revenue stream requires a nuanced understanding of several key factors including audience demographics, engagement metrics, and content optimization strategies.

- Audience Demographics: Advertisers are keen on targeting specific demographics, making it crucial for creators to understand their audience deeply. Content tailored towards a particular age group, geographic location, or interest can attract higher-paying ads.

- Engagement Metrics: Higher engagement rates such as likes, comments, and shares can increase a video's visibility and its attractiveness to advertisers. Engaging content that prompts viewer interaction is more likely to be prioritized by YouTube's algorithm.

- Content Optimization: Utilizing SEO techniques not only enhances discoverability but also improves ad relevancy. Keywords, tags, and compelling thumbnails play a significant role in attracting both viewers and relevant advertisements.

Beyond these foundational aspects, exploring alternative advertising formats such as sponsored content, product placements within videos, or direct collaborations with brands can open additional revenue streams. These alternatives require creators to maintain a delicate balance between monetization and providing value-driven content that resonates with their audience.

In conclusion, while ad revenue presents an attractive monetization avenue for adult YouTubers looking to grow their channels and income simultaneously, it demands strategic planning and continuous adaptation to changing trends and policies. Creators who invest time in understanding the intricacies of ad-based monetization are better positioned to maximize their earnings while fostering a loyal viewer base.

6.2 Diversifying Income through Sponsorships and Merchandise

Diversifying income streams is a critical strategy for content creators aiming to achieve financial stability and growth. Beyond the foundational ad revenue, sponsorships and merchandise offer potent avenues for enhancing earnings. This section delves into how creators can effectively leverage these opportunities to build a more resilient financial model.

Sponsorships play a pivotal role in diversification, allowing creators to partner with brands that resonate with their audience. These collaborations range from simple product mentions to comprehensive brand integrations within content. The key to successful sponsorships lies in aligning with brands that share similar values and appeal to the creator's audience, ensuring authenticity in promotion.

- Identifying Potential Sponsors: Creators should seek out companies whose products or services they genuinely appreciate. This authenticity translates into more engaging promotions that audiences can trust.
- Negotiating Terms: Understanding one's value is crucial when entering negotiations with potential sponsors. Creators should consider their reach, engagement rates, and audience demographics to propose fair compensation.
- Maintaining Transparency: It's essential for creators to disclose sponsored content clearly, adhering to regulatory guidelines and maintaining trust with their audience.

Merchandising offers another lucrative stream of income, enabling creators to sell branded products directly to their fans. From apparel and accessories to digital goods like eBooks or courses, merchandise can significantly boost a creator's earnings while also strengthening the community around their brand.

In conclusion, diversifying income through sponsorships and merchandise not only enhances a creator's earning potential but also builds deeper connections with their audience by offering value beyond content alone. By strategically selecting partners and products that align with their brand identity and audience preferences, creators can establish sustainable revenue streams while maintaining authenticity and trust.

- Product Selection: Choosing merchandise that reflects the creator's brand identity and resonates with their audience is vital. Custom designs or products related to popular content can perform exceptionally well.

- E-commerce Platforms: Utilizing online platforms like Shopify or integrating merch stores directly into social media profiles simplifies the selling process for both creators and buyers.

- Promotion Strategies: Effective marketing of merchandise through social media teasers, exclusive offers for subscribers, or showcasing products in videos can drive sales significantly.

6.3 Leveraging Membership Platforms

In the evolving landscape of digital content creation, leveraging membership platforms emerges as a strategic approach to monetize and deepen audience engagement. Unlike traditional revenue streams, membership platforms offer a unique opportunity for creators to build a sustainable income by providing exclusive content, experiences, or perks to their subscribers. This model not only diversifies income but also fosters a stronger community around the creator's brand.

Membership platforms such as Patreon, Memberful, or Substack allow creators to set up subscription-based services where fans pay a recurring fee for access to premium content. This could range from behind-the-scenes footage, early access to content, members-only posts, newsletters, or even physical merchandise. The key advantage here is the ability to create a predictable and steady stream of income that is directly proportional to the creator's effort in engaging their subscriber base.

- Community Building: At its core, successful use of membership platforms hinges on the ability to cultivate an engaged community. Creators must consistently deliver value that exceeds the monetary cost of membership, encouraging loyalty and long-term support.
- Exclusive Content: Offering content that is exclusive to members can significantly enhance perceived value. This requires understanding what aspects of your work or insights your audience is most willing to pay for.
- Pricing Strategies: Setting appropriate subscription tiers is crucial. Creators should offer multiple levels of membership to cater to different segments of their audience, from casual fans to more dedicated supporters.

Beyond financial benefits, membership platforms provide an intimate space for creators to interact with their most dedicated followers. This direct line of communication allows for immediate feedback and fosters a sense of ownership among members over the creator's work. Moreover, it enables creators to experiment with new ideas or projects with the backing of a supportive community.

In conclusion, leveraging membership platforms represents a powerful strategy for creators looking to monetize their content while building meaningful relationships with their audience. By offering exclusive content and experiences in exchange for recurring support, creators can achieve greater financial stability and independence. However, success in this arena demands commitment to delivering consistent value and maintaining an active engagement with the member community.

References:

- Patreon. (n.d.). How to Start a Patreon & Make Money as a Creator. Retrieved from https://www.patreon.com/
- Memberful. (n.d.). Professional membership software used by the web's biggest creators. Retrieved from https://memberful.com/
- Substack. (n.d.). Substack makes it simple for a writer to start an email newsletter that makes money from subscriptions. Retrieved from https://substack.com/
- Carr, D. (2020). The Creator Economy: How People Are Turning Their Passions Into Profits. Forbes. Retrieved from https://www.forbes.com/

7

Building a Community on YouTube

7.1 Engaging with Your Audience Effectively

Engaging with your audience is not just about responding to comments or asking viewers to like and subscribe; it's about building a genuine connection that fosters community and loyalty around your channel. This section delves into the nuances of effective audience engagement, offering insights beyond conventional wisdom to help you cultivate a vibrant and interactive community on YouTube.

Firstly, understanding your audience is paramount. This involves analyzing viewer demographics, preferences, and feedback to tailor your content and interaction strategies accordingly. Creating content that resonates with your audience's interests, challenges, and aspirations can significantly enhance engagement levels.

Secondly, leveraging social media platforms to extend the conversation outside of YouTube can provide a more rounded community experience. Platforms like Twitter, Instagram, and Facebook allow for different types of interactions, from behind-the-scenes glimpses to real-time discussions, making your presence felt across the digital landscape.

- Personalized Responses: Taking the time to craft personalized replies to comments shows that you value viewer input and fosters a welcoming environment.
- Community Posts: Utilize YouTube's Community tab to share updates, polls, or questions that stimulate interaction and keep your audience engaged between video uploads.
- Live Q&A Sessions: Hosting live sessions can humanize your online persona and provide an opportunity for real-time engagement. It allows for immediate feedback and creates a sense of event around your content.

Incorporating user-generated content (UGC) such as fan art, stories, or video responses into your videos or community posts can also significantly boost engagement by making viewers feel directly involved in the channel's content creation process. Highlighting UGC not only rewards creative contributions but also encourages others in the community to participate actively.

Finally, consistency in communication style and frequency helps set expectations for when and how interactions occur on your channel. Whether through regular comment response times or scheduled live streams, maintaining a consistent presence reassures your audience of your commitment to the community you're building together.

In conclusion, engaging with your audience effectively requires a multifaceted approach that goes beyond mere interaction. It's about creating meaningful connections through tailored content, extending interactions across platforms, incorporating viewer contributions, and maintaining consistent communication practices. By adopting these strategies, you can foster a loyal community that supports sustained growth on YouTube.

7.2 Encouraging Viewer Loyalty

Encouraging viewer loyalty is a critical aspect of building a sustainable community on YouTube. It goes beyond the initial engagement to create a lasting relationship with your audience, turning casual viewers into dedicated fans. This section explores strategies to foster loyalty and ensure viewers keep coming back for more.

Understanding the psychological underpinnings of viewer loyalty is essential. People tend to gravitate towards channels that consistently provide value, whether through entertainment, education, or emotional connection. Thus, creating content that consistently meets or exceeds expectations is foundational in encouraging loyalty.

Recognition plays a significant role in fostering viewer loyalty. Acknowledging viewers through shoutouts, featuring their comments in videos or live streams, and responding to their feedback makes them feel valued and part of the channel's community. This personal touch can significantly enhance their sense of belonging and commitment to your channel.

- Exclusive Content: Offering exclusive content or early access to videos for subscribers can make them feel privileged and appreciated, increasing their loyalty.
- Loyalty Rewards: Implementing a system where viewers earn rewards for their engagement (e.g., exclusive badges or custom emojis) can incentivize continued support.
- Consistent Engagement: Regularly engaging with your audience through comments, social media, and community posts keeps the conversation going and strengthens relationships.

Incorporating storytelling into your content strategy can also be a powerful tool in building loyalty. Sharing personal stories or behind-the-scenes looks into your life creates transparency and trust, making viewers feel more connected to you as a creator.

Maintaining consistency in upload schedules helps set clear expectations for your audience about when they can look forward to new content. This regularity not only aids in habit formation but also builds anticipation among viewers, keeping them engaged over time.

To conclude, encouraging viewer loyalty requires a multifaceted approach that includes understanding audience needs, recognizing their contributions, providing exclusive benefits, engaging consistently, leveraging storytelling, and maintaining a reliable content schedule. By implementing these strategies effectively, creators can cultivate a loyal community that supports long-term channel growth on YouTube.

7.3 Managing Comments and Feedback

Managing comments and feedback is a pivotal aspect of nurturing a vibrant community on YouTube. This process not only involves moderating comments to maintain a positive environment but also engaging with your audience to foster a sense of belonging and loyalty. Effective management of this interaction can significantly impact the growth and sustainability of your channel.

Firstly, it's crucial to establish clear guidelines for your community to follow when commenting. These rules should promote respectful and constructive dialogue, discouraging any form of negativity or harassment. By setting these expectations early on, you create a safer space for viewers to express their thoughts and opinions.

Engagement is the heart of managing comments and feedback. Responding to comments, whether they are questions, compliments, or constructive criticism, shows that you value your audience's input. This two-way communication not only enhances viewer satisfaction but also encourages more interaction, which can boost your video's visibility through YouTube's algorithm.

- Moderation Tools: Utilize YouTube's built-in moderation tools to filter out spam or inappropriate comments automatically. This helps maintain the quality of discussions under your videos without requiring constant manual oversight.

- Pinned Comments: Highlighting positive or informative comments by pinning them at the top of the comment section can guide the conversation in a positive direction and showcase the best of your community.

- Community Moderators: Appointing trusted members from your audience as moderators can help manage large volumes of comments more effectively. They can assist in enforcing community guidelines and maintaining a respectful dialogue.

Incorporating feedback into your content creation process is another vital component. Listening to what your viewers have to say about your videos can provide valuable insights into their preferences and interests. This information can guide future content decisions, making your channel more attuned to its audience's needs.

To conclude, managing comments and feedback is an ongoing task that requires attention and dedication. However, by fostering positive interactions, setting clear guidelines, utilizing moderation tools effectively, and incorporating viewer feedback into content planning, creators can build stronger connections with their audience. These efforts contribute significantly towards developing a loyal community around your YouTube channel.

References:

- YouTube Help - Manage comments and feedback: A comprehensive guide by YouTube on how to effectively manage comments and engage with your audience.

- Creator Academy - Building a Community: YouTube's Creator Academy offers insights and tips on fostering a positive community, including managing comments and feedback.

- Social Media Examiner - How to Manage YouTube Comments: An article providing strategies for handling comments on YouTube, including the use of moderation tools and engaging with viewers.

- Hootsuite Blog - The Complete Guide to YouTube Marketing in 2023: This guide includes a section on managing community engagement and feedback on YouTube, highlighting best practices for creators.

8

Navigating Challenges as an Adult YouTuber

8.1 Dealing with Criticism and Negative Comments

Entering the world of YouTube as an adult content creator comes with its unique set of challenges, among which dealing with criticism and negative comments stands out significantly. This aspect is crucial for maintaining mental well-being and ensuring sustained growth on the platform. Understanding how to navigate through negative feedback without letting it hinder your progress is essential for anyone looking to make a mark in the digital space.

Criticism, when constructive, can be a valuable tool for improvement. It offers insights into how your content is perceived from an audience's perspective, highlighting areas that may need refinement or adjustment. However, not all criticism is constructive; YouTube, like any other social media platform, has its share of unconstructive negativity and trolling. The key lies in differentiating between feedback that is meant to guide and comments that serve no purpose other than to disparage.

Navigating through criticism requires resilience but also presents an opportunity for personal and professional development. By embracing constructive feedback while shielding oneself from unwarranted negativity, adult YouTubers can cultivate a healthy relationship with their audience, laying down a foundation for long-term success on the platform.

- Identify Constructive Criticism: Learn to distinguish between comments that offer genuine feedback and those that are purely negative. This discernment helps in focusing on inputs that can actually enhance your content quality.

- Maintain Professionalism: Responding to criticism with professionalism keeps the conversation productive and reflects positively on you as a creator. It shows your commitment to growth and respect towards your audience.

- Utilize Feedback Loops: Implementing a system to regularly gather and analyze viewer feedback can turn criticisms into actionable insights, driving continuous improvement in content creation.

- Create Boundaries: While engagement is key to building a community around your channel, setting boundaries for acceptable interactions helps safeguard against the impact of negative comments.

- Foster a Supportive Community: Encouraging positive interaction within your comment section can create an environment where constructive feedback thrives over negativity.

8.2 Managing Privacy Concerns Online

In the digital age, where personal and professional lives often intersect on platforms like YouTube, managing privacy concerns becomes a paramount challenge for adult content creators. The nature of their content can attract unwarranted attention, making it crucial to navigate the thin line between public persona and private life meticulously. This section delves into strategies for safeguarding personal information, handling doxxing threats, and creating a secure online environment.

Firstly, understanding the platform's privacy settings is fundamental. YouTube offers various tools that allow creators to control who sees their content and how interactions are managed. Familiarizing oneself with these options can prevent unwanted exposure. However, technical settings alone are not enough; creators must also be mindful of the information they share in videos and social media. Subtle details like background locations or inadvertently revealed personal details can lead to privacy breaches.

- Use Pseudonyms: Adopting a stage name or pseudonym helps separate your public persona from your private identity, adding a layer of anonymity that can protect against doxxing attempts.

- Avoid Sharing Personal Information: Be cautious about revealing identifiable information such as addresses, phone numbers, or even birthdays. Remember that seemingly innocuous details can be pieced together by malicious individuals.

- Engage Legal Resources: In cases where privacy breaches occur or personal safety is threatened, understanding legal rights and resources available for protection is crucial. This may include copyright laws, restraining orders, or seeking assistance from law enforcement.

Beyond individual efforts to maintain privacy, fostering a community culture that respects boundaries is equally important. Encouraging respectful interaction and discouraging invasive curiosity among viewers can help create a safer space for both creators and fans alike. Additionally, collaborating with other YouTubers who share similar concerns can provide mutual support and exchange of best practices in privacy management.

In conclusion, while the internet offers unprecedented opportunities for expression and connection, it also poses significant risks to personal privacy. Adult YouTubers face unique challenges in this realm but through careful management of online presence, utilization of platform tools for privacy protection, and fostering a respectful community culture, they can navigate these waters successfully.

Balancing openness with caution allows creators to share their work without compromising their safety or well-being.

8.3 Staying Motivated During Slow Growth Periods

For adult YouTubers, encountering periods of slow growth is an inevitable part of the journey. These phases can be disheartening, leading to a decline in motivation and even causing some creators to question their path. However, understanding how to navigate these times effectively can not only help in maintaining motivation but also in laying the groundwork for future success.

The first step in staying motivated during slow growth periods is setting realistic expectations. Understanding that growth on platforms like YouTube is rarely linear helps put these slower phases into perspective. It's important for creators to recognize that every channel experiences fluctuations in growth due to various factors such as changes in algorithm, viewer behavior, or market saturation.

- Reflect and Reassess: Use this time as an opportunity to reflect on your content strategy. Analyze which videos perform well and why, then consider experimenting with new content ideas or formats that could appeal to your target audience.

- Engage with Your Community: Even if growth is slow, engaging with your existing audience can provide valuable feedback and foster a loyal community. This engagement can be through responding to comments, hosting live Q&A sessions, or creating content based on viewer suggestions.

- Invest in Learning: Slow periods are an excellent time for personal and professional development. Learning new skills such as video editing techniques, SEO strategies for YouTube, or even studying trends within the adult content niche can enhance the quality of your content and prepare you for future growth.

Beyond these practical steps, finding intrinsic motivation by remembering why you started creating content in the first place can be powerful. Whether it was to express yourself creatively, share knowledge, or connect with others who have similar interests, reconnecting with your initial motivations can reignite passion during challenging times.

In conclusion, while slow growth periods are challenging for adult YouTubers, they also offer opportunities for reflection, community building, skill development, and reconnection with one's core motivations. By adopting a proactive approach and leveraging these strategies, creators can maintain their motivation and position themselves for success when growth accelerates once again.

References:

- YouTube Creator Academy: Discoverability - Offers insights into how YouTube's algorithm works and tips for increasing your channel's visibility.

- TubeFilter - Provides the latest news on social video platforms, including trends and analysis that can help creators stay ahead of the curve.

- VidIQ Blog: How to Grow Your YouTube Channel - Features strategies for growth on YouTube, including SEO best practices and content creation tips.

- Social Media Examiner: YouTube Growth Tips - Offers advice from successful YouTubers on how to grow your channel and engage with your audience effectively.

9

Advanced Video Production Techniques

9.1 Lighting and Sound Optimization

Lighting and sound optimization are crucial elements in the production of high-quality YouTube videos, especially for adults looking to grow their channel and engage a mature audience effectively. Proper lighting ensures that the subject is well-lit, making the video more visually appealing and professional. On the other hand, clear and crisp sound quality can significantly enhance viewer experience, encouraging longer watch times and higher engagement rates.

When it comes to lighting, three-point lighting is a fundamental setup that can dramatically improve video quality. This setup includes a key light, which is the primary source of light directed at the subject; a fill light, which reduces shadows caused by the key light; and a back light, which helps separate the subject from the background. Utilizing natural light can also be beneficial, but it requires careful timing and positioning to ensure consistency throughout filming.

Sound optimization involves several techniques to achieve clear audio. The first step is selecting an appropriate microphone that suits your recording environment and content type. Lapel microphones are great for direct-to-camera presentations, while shotgun mics may be better suited for dynamic shooting scenarios. Additionally, recording in a quiet space with minimal echo can drastically improve sound quality. Using acoustic panels or even soft furnishings can help absorb unwanted sound reflections within indoor environments.

- Understanding different lighting setups and their impact on video aesthetics.
- Selecting microphones based on content needs and recording conditions.
- Implementing strategies to minimize background noise and echo for clearer audio recordings.

In conclusion, mastering lighting and sound optimization not only enhances the technical quality of videos but also contributes to creating content that resonates with viewers on a deeper level. By investing time in learning these skills, adult YouTubers can produce content that stands out in a crowded digital landscape, fostering growth and building a loyal community around their channel.

9.2 Advanced Editing Skills

Following the foundational aspects of lighting and sound optimization, advanced editing skills become the linchpin in transforming raw footage into compelling content. This section delves into the nuanced techniques that elevate a video's storytelling capability, engagement factor, and overall production value. Advanced editing encompasses a broad spectrum of skills from color grading to pacing and rhythm, each playing a pivotal role in captivating an audience.

Color grading stands out as one of the most transformative editing techniques. It involves adjusting the colors in your video to achieve a specific look or mood. This can range from creating a warm, inviting atmosphere for lifestyle content to employing a cool, desaturated color scheme for dramatic effect. Mastery over color grading not only enhances visual appeal but also reinforces the narrative tone of your content.

Another critical aspect is pacing and rhythm, which dictate how effectively a video maintains viewer interest. Skilled editors manipulate clip lengths, transitions, and timing to ensure that each segment contributes to a cohesive flow. Strategic cuts and transitions are employed not just for aesthetic purposes but to guide viewers through the story seamlessly. For instance, rapid cuts might be used in high-energy sequences to keep adrenaline levels high, while longer takes can immerse viewers in more introspective moments.

- Utilizing J-cuts and L-cuts to create smooth transitions between scenes that enhance narrative cohesion.
- Incorporating motion graphics and visual effects judiciously to add depth or highlight key points without overwhelming the primary message.
- Employing sound design techniques such as layering ambient sounds or music tracks to build an immersive

audio environment that complements the visual experience.

Beyond these techniques, advanced editing also involves a keen sense of storytelling. Editors must choose which shots best convey the intended message or emotion and arrange them in a way that maximizes impact on the viewer. This decision-making process is crucial in crafting content that resonates deeply with audiences, making advanced editing skills indispensable for any aspiring video creator aiming for professional-grade productions.

In conclusion, mastering advanced editing skills requires both technical proficiency and artistic sensibility. By combining sophisticated color grading with thoughtful pacing and innovative use of sound and visuals, editors can transform simple footage into engaging narratives that captivate viewers from start to finish.

9.3 Creating a Consistent Brand Aesthetic

Creating a consistent brand aesthetic in video production is not just about maintaining uniformity in visual elements; it's about crafting a cohesive narrative that resonates with your audience across all content. This consistency is crucial for building brand recognition and loyalty, as it helps viewers instantly connect the content with your brand, regardless of the platform or format.

The first step towards achieving this consistency is defining your brand's visual identity. This includes selecting specific color schemes, fonts, logos, and even thematic elements that align with your brand's values and message. Once established, these elements should be consistently applied across all video content to reinforce brand identity.

- Implementing a style guide that outlines the use of visual elements such as logos, color palettes, and typography ensures uniformity across productions.

- Choosing a consistent tone and mood for your videos can also help solidify your brandâ€™s aesthetic. Whether itâ€™s inspirational, humorous, or professional, sticking to a specific tone makes your content immediately recognizable.

- Incorporating recurring motifs or themes can further enhance brand continuity. These could be visual symbols, narrative elements, or even specific audio cues that become synonymous with your brand.

Beyond visuals, the narrative structure of your videos plays a significant role in creating a consistent brand aesthetic. Crafting stories that align with your brand's core values not only strengthens the overall message but also fosters an emotional connection with the audience. This storytelling approach should be adapted to fit various platforms while maintaining the essence of your brand's message.

Finally, consistency in quality cannot be overlooked. High production values signal professionalism and dedication to excellence which reflects positively on the perception of your brand. Investing in good lighting, sound optimization (as discussed in previous sections), and advanced editing skills ensures that each piece of content meets a high standard of quality that audiences will come to expect from your brand.

In conclusion, creating a consistent brand aesthetic requires meticulous planning and execution across various aspects of video production. By establishing clear guidelines for visual identity, tone, storytelling, and quality—and applying them uniformly—you can craft compelling content that strengthens your brand's presence in the digital landscape.

References:

- Why A Consistent Brand Matters And How To Achieve It - Forbes
- The Importance of Building a Strong Brand Image - Entrepreneur
- The Ultimate Guide to Branding in 2022 - HubSpot
- A Complete Guide to Creating an Awesome Brand Aesthetic for Social Media - Buffer

10

Social Media Integration and Cross-Promotion

1.1 Utilizing Social Media to Boost Visibility

In the realm of digital content creation, particularly for adults venturing into YouTube, leveraging social media platforms is a critical strategy for amplifying visibility and engagement. This approach transcends mere content sharing; it involves a nuanced understanding of different social media ecosystems and how they can synergize to elevate a creator's presence online. The essence of utilizing social media lies in its ability to connect creators with their audience beyond YouTube, fostering a multi-platform community that thrives on interaction and shared values.

One fundamental aspect of this strategy is identifying which social media platforms harbor the target demographic. For adult creators, platforms like LinkedIn, Twitter, and Facebook might offer more direct access to an audience that appreciates nuanced discussions or professional content. Instagram and TikTok, while skewing towards a younger demographic, can also be valuable for visual storytelling and reaching a broader audience interested in lifestyle or creative niches.

- Creating platform-specific content that complements YouTube videos encourages followers to engage across multiple channels.
- Strategic use of hashtags and trends on platforms like Instagram and Twitter can significantly increase discoverability among users not yet familiar with one's YouTube channel.
- Engaging directly with followers through comments, live sessions, and Q&As on various platforms builds a sense of community and loyalty around the creator's brand.

Beyond individual platform tactics, cross-promotion plays a pivotal role in utilizing social media effectively. This involves not just sharing links to new videos but creating value-added interactions for followers. For instance, offering behind-the-scenes looks on Instagram Stories or conducting Twitter polls to decide on future video topics can make followers feel involved in the creative process. Additionally, collaborating with other creators across social media platforms can expose one's channel to diverse audiences, facilitating organic growth through shared visibility.

In conclusion, harnessing the power of social media for boosting visibility requires more than sporadic posts across different platforms; it demands a strategic approach tailored to each platform's strengths and audience preferences. By engaging authentically with their community across these spaces, adult YouTubers can significantly enhance their channel's reach and impact in the crowded digital landscape.

10.2 Collaborations with Other Creators

Collaborating with other creators stands as a cornerstone strategy for amplifying one's visibility and engagement across social media platforms. This approach not only diversifies content but also merges distinct audiences, creating a symbiotic relationship that benefits all parties involved. The essence of successful collaborations lies in the strategic selection of partners whose audience demographics, content themes, and brand values align closely with one's own.

Effective collaborations go beyond mere cross-promotion; they involve co-creating content that is unique, engaging, and offers added value to the combined audience base. This could range from guest appearances on each other's YouTube channels to joint live streams on platforms like Instagram or Twitch, where real-time interaction can significantly enhance viewer engagement. Moreover, collaborative projects such as challenges, giveaways, or charity events can generate substantial buzz and foster a sense of community among followers.

- Identifying potential collaborators by analyzing audience overlap and complementary content niches ensures mutual benefit.
- Planning collaborative content that leverages the unique strengths and perspectives of each creator can lead to innovative and compelling outputs.

- Maintaining open communication and setting clear expectations from the outset helps in managing collaborative projects smoothly.

In addition to these direct benefits, collaborations often lead to informal knowledge exchanges between creators. Insights into best practices for content creation, audience engagement strategies, or even technical aspects like video editing can be invaluable. These interactions foster a supportive creator community where shared learning accelerates individual growth.

In conclusion, leveraging collaborations with other creators represents a powerful strategy for expanding one's digital footprint across social media landscapes. By carefully selecting partners and creatively integrating their strengths into joint projects, creators can unlock new levels of visibility and audience engagement while contributing to a vibrant online community.

To maximize the impact of collaborations, it is crucial to promote these partnerships across all social media channels involved. Tailoring the promotional content to fit each platform's unique format and audience preferences can further boost reach and effectiveness. Post-collaboration analysis through metrics such as engagement rates, subscriber growth, or video views provides valuable feedback for refining future collaborative efforts.

10.3 Effective Cross-Promotion Strategies

Building on the foundation of collaborations with other creators, effective cross-promotion strategies serve as a pivotal mechanism for amplifying reach and engagement across diverse social media platforms. This approach leverages the combined strengths of different channels and creators to maximize visibility and audience interaction. The essence of successful cross-promotion lies in the strategic alignment of content, timing, and messaging to resonate with a broader yet targeted audience.

Cross-promotion transcends simple shout-outs or mentions. It involves a carefully orchestrated campaign where each party contributes unique content that complements the overall theme and objectives of the collaboration. For instance, a series of interconnected posts across Instagram, Twitter, Facebook, and YouTube can tell a cohesive story or highlight different facets of a joint venture, such as a product launch or an event. This multi-platform narrative engages audiences more deeply by offering varied yet consistent touchpoints.

- Timing is crucial in cross-promotion; synchronizing content releases across platforms maximizes exposure and impact.

- Customizing content to suit the format and audience preferences of each platform enhances relevance and engagement.

- Utilizing analytics tools to track performance across platforms provides insights into audience behavior and preferences, enabling more targeted future collaborations.

In addition to leveraging digital platforms, effective cross-promotion strategies often incorporate offline elements such as QR codes in physical locations or live events that encourage online interaction. This blend of online and offline tactics enriches the audience's experience and broadens the scope of engagement opportunities.

Moreover, transparency about the collaborative nature of cross-promotions fosters authenticity and trust among audiences. Clearly communicating the mutual benefits and shared values underlying a partnership resonates with consumers' desire for genuine connections with brands and creators.

In conclusion, effective cross-promotion strategies require meticulous planning, creative execution, and ongoing optimization based on performance data. By embracing these principles, creators can significantly extend their reach, deepen audience engagement, and forge stronger relationships with fellow creatorsâ€"ultimately contributing to sustained growth in an ever-evolving digital landscape.

References:

- Smith, J. (2022). "Maximizing Your Social Media Strategy Through Cross-Promotion." Digital Marketing Insights Journal.

- Jones, A., & Lee, M. (2021). "The Power of Collaboration: Enhancing Brand Visibility Across Platforms." Social Media Today.

- Brown, K. (2023). "Leveraging Analytics for Effective Cross-Platform Campaigns." Analytics in Action Review.

- Green, L. (2020). "Integrating Offline and Online Marketing Efforts for Comprehensive Campaigns." Modern Marketing Quarterly.

- Davis, R. (2019). "Building Authentic Brand Partnerships in the Digital Age." Brand Integrity International.

11

Analytics and Performance Tracking

1.1 Setting Up YouTube Analytics

Understanding and leveraging YouTube Analytics is crucial for anyone looking to grow their channel, especially for adults venturing into content creation with the aim of sharing their passions, transitioning careers, or generating an additional income stream. This section delves into the initial steps required to set up and navigate YouTube Analytics, providing a foundation for creators to analyze performance, understand their audience better, and make informed decisions that align with their growth strategies.

The process begins by ensuring that you have a YouTube channel linked to a Google account. Once this basic requirement is met, access to YouTube Studio becomes available, which is the hub for managing your content and where YouTube Analytics can be found. The analytics section offers a comprehensive overview of various metrics critical to channel growth such as watch time, viewer demographics, traffic sources, and engagement rates.

In conclusion, setting up YouTube Analytics is a foundational step towards building a successful YouTube channel as an adult creator. By effectively utilizing these tools from the outset, creators can gain invaluable insights into their channel's performance and audience behavior. This not only aids in refining content strategies but also enhances engagement and fosters community building around one's channel. As part of a broader strategy outlined in "How To Grow On YouTube As An Adult," mastering YouTube Analytics empowers creators to navigate through challenges with data-driven confidence.

- Activating Advanced Features: To fully utilize analytics tools, creators must verify their account and enable advanced features. This step unlocks additional metrics and functionalities that are indispensable for detailed analysis.

- Navigating the Dashboard: Familiarizing yourself with the dashboard is key. It provides a snapshot of your channel's performance including recent uploads' performance, real-time activity, and personalized insights based on your content's performance.

- Understanding Key Metrics: Delving deeper into analytics involves understanding what each metric represents and how it impacts your channel. For instance, knowing the difference between impressions and engagement can help tailor content strategy more effectively.

- Audience Insights: One of the most valuable aspects of YouTube Analytics is its ability to provide detailed insights into who your viewers are - including age groups, geographical locations, and viewing preferences. This information is instrumental in creating targeted content that resonates with your audience.

11.2 Interpreting Data to Guide Strategy

In the realm of digital content creation, particularly on platforms like YouTube, the ability to interpret analytics data is not just beneficialâ€"it's essential for strategic growth. This section delves into how creators can leverage data insights to refine their content strategy, enhance viewer engagement, and ultimately achieve their channel objectives more effectively.

At its core, interpreting data involves moving beyond surface-level metrics to understand the story behind the numbers. For instance, a sudden spike in viewership might indicate that a particular topic or format resonates with your audience. Conversely, a decline could signal content fatigue or a mismatch between your videos and viewer preferences. By analyzing these trends over time, creators can identify patterns that inform future content decisions.

- Demographic Insights: Understanding who watches your content is as crucial as knowing how many people watch it. Analytics can reveal detailed demographic information such as age ranges, geographical locations, and even preferred viewing times. This information allows creators to tailor their content and posting schedule to better match their audience's profile.

- Engagement Metrics: Engagement goes beyond views; it encompasses likes, comments, shares, and watch time. High engagement rates often indicate that viewers find your content valuable enough to interact with it or watch it through to the end. Analyzing which videos garner the most engagement can guide creators in producing more of what their audience loves.

- Traffic Sources: Knowing where your viewers come from—be it search results, direct links, or recommended videos—can help you understand how discoverable your content is on YouTube and other platforms. This insight is invaluable for optimizing video titles, descriptions, and tags for SEO and exploring promotional strategies outside of YouTube.

To effectively interpret data and apply these insights to your strategy requires regular review and adaptation. The digital landscape evolves rapidly; what works today may not work tomorrow. Therefore, successful creators are those who remain flexible in their approach—constantly learning from their analytics to create more engaging and relevant content for their audience.

In conclusion, interpreting analytics data empowers YouTube creators with the knowledge needed to make informed decisions about their content strategy. By understanding viewer behavior and preferences at a granular level, creators can enhance engagement, grow their audience base, and achieve greater success on the platform.

11.3 Adjusting Content Based on Performance Insights

Understanding and interpreting analytics is a crucial step in content creation, but the real power lies in using those insights to adjust and optimize future content. This process involves a detailed analysis of performance metrics to identify what resonates with the audience and what doesn't. By closely monitoring these insights, creators can make informed decisions that enhance viewer engagement, improve content relevance, and ultimately drive channel growth.

The first step in this process is identifying key performance indicators (KPIs) such as view count, watch time, engagement rate (likes, comments, shares), and subscriber growth. These metrics provide a quantitative measure of content performance. However, the qualitative analysis—understanding why certain content performs better—is equally important. This might involve reviewing viewer comments for feedback or noting the context around spikes in viewership (such as trending topics or external events).

- Content Optimization: Based on performance data, creators can tweak their content strategy to focus more on topics, formats, or styles that have proven successful. For instance, if how-to videos receive significantly higher engagement than vlogs, it might be beneficial to produce more instructional content.

- Audience Alignment: Demographic insights allow creators to tailor their content to better suit their audience's preferences. If analytics reveal a predominantly young audience interested in technology, incorporating the latest tech trends into videos could increase relevance and viewer retention.

- SEO Adjustments: Analyzing traffic sources can highlight opportunities for improving video discoverability through search engine optimization (SEO). Creators might adjust video titles, descriptions, or tags based on keywords that are driving views or explore new promotional channels to reach potential viewers.

Incorporating feedback loops where audience input directly influences future content creation is another effective strategy for adjusting based on performance insights. Engaging with viewers through comments or polls can provide direct feedback that guides content adjustments.

To stay ahead in the dynamic landscape of digital media, creators must be willing to continuously learn from their analytics and adapt their strategies accordingly. This iterative process of creating content, analyzing performance, making adjustments based on insights gathered—and then repeating the cycle—ensures sustained growth and relevance in an ever-evolving market.

References:

- YouTube Creator Academy. "Understand Your Channel Analytics." Offers comprehensive guides on interpreting and utilizing YouTube analytics to improve content strategy.

- Google Analytics Help Center. "Beginner's Guide to Google Analytics." Provides insights into how to use

Google Analytics for website and content performance analysis.

- Hootsuite Blog. "Social Media Metrics That Matter." Highlights key social media performance metrics and how to use them for content optimization.

- Content Marketing Institute. "How to Use Content Marketing Analytics & Data." Discusses the importance of data in content marketing and strategies for using analytics to drive content decisions.

12

Future Trends in Digital Content Creation

1.1 Emerging Technologies Impacting YouTube

The landscape of digital content creation is perpetually evolving, with emerging technologies playing a pivotal role in shaping how content is produced, distributed, and consumed on platforms like YouTube. These advancements not only offer new opportunities for creators but also challenge them to adapt and innovate to stay relevant in a competitive space.

One significant technology impacting YouTube is Artificial Intelligence (AI). AI-driven tools are revolutionizing video editing, making it more efficient and accessible. Automated editing software can now analyze footage and make smart cuts, add transitions, and even suggest content improvements based on viewer engagement data. This democratizes high-quality video production, enabling creators with limited technical skills to produce polished content that resonates with audiences.

Another area where technology is making its mark is through Virtual Reality (VR) and Augmented Reality (AR). These immersive technologies are opening up new avenues for content creation on YouTube. Creators can now produce 360-degree videos that offer viewers an interactive experience, transporting them to virtual environments or augmenting the real world with digital overlays. This has implications not just for entertainment content but also for educational and instructional videos, providing a more engaging learning experience.

In addition to these technologies, the rise of live streaming on YouTube presents both challenges and opportunities. Real-time interaction capabilities demand creators to master new skills such as engaging with live comments while maintaining the flow of their presentation. However, this immediacy also fosters a stronger connection between creators and their audience, offering unique opportunities for community building.

- AI-driven analytics tools help creators understand audience preferences in greater depth, allowing for more targeted content strategies.

- Blockchain technology offers potential solutions for copyright issues, enabling more secure and transparent content monetization mechanisms.

- Advanced drones and camera stabilizing equipment are enhancing the quality of aerial videography and action shots, expanding the possibilities for adventure and travel vloggers.

The integration of these emerging technologies into YouTube's ecosystem not only enriches the viewer experience but also empowers creators to explore innovative storytelling techniques. As these technologies continue to evolve, they will undoubtedly shape the future trends in digital content creation on YouTube, challenging creators to continually adapt their strategies to leverage these advancements effectively.

12.2 Adapting to Changes in Viewer Behavior

The digital landscape is witnessing a seismic shift in viewer behavior, driven by technological advancements and changing consumer preferences. This evolution presents both a challenge and an opportunity for content creators on platforms like YouTube, necessitating a strategic pivot to align with these new consumption patterns. Understanding and adapting to these changes is crucial for creators aiming to maintain and grow their audience base.

One of the most significant shifts has been the move towards mobile consumption. Viewers are increasingly accessing content on-the-go, favoring smartphones over traditional desktop setups. This transition demands that creators optimize their content for mobile viewing, considering factors such as screen size and video length. Short-form content, exemplified by platforms like TikTok, has surged in popularity, suggesting that YouTube creators may need to explore more concise formats or segments within longer videos to capture and retain viewer attention.

Another key trend is the demand for authenticity and relatability in content. Modern viewers gravitate towards creators who share personal stories or take stands on social issues, reflecting a broader desire for genuine connection rather than polished perfection. This shift underscores the importance of personal branding and narrative storytelling in content creation strategies.

- Interactive features such as polls, live streaming, and community posts have become vital tools for engaging with audiences directly on YouTube. These features not only enhance viewer engagement but also provide valuable feedback mechanisms for creators to fine-tune their content based on real-time reactions.
- The rise of niche communities offers opportunities for creators to cater to specific interests or demographics, emphasizing depth over breadth in audience engagement strategies.
- Data-driven decision-making is increasingly important, with AI-powered analytics tools enabling creators to understand viewer preferences more deeply and tailor their content accordingly.

In conclusion, adapting to changes in viewer behavior requires a multifaceted approach that embraces technological innovation while staying true to authentic storytelling principles. By leveraging data analytics for insights into audience preferences and experimenting with interactive formats and mobile-optimized content, creators can navigate the evolving digital landscape successfully. The future of digital content creation lies in understanding these behavioral shifts and responding creatively and strategically.

12.3 Planning for Long-Term Growth on the Platform

As digital content creation evolves, planning for long-term growth on platforms like YouTube becomes increasingly critical. This strategic planning involves not just adapting to current trends but also forecasting future shifts in viewer behavior and platform algorithms. A sustainable growth strategy encompasses a deep understanding of content optimization, audience engagement, and brand evolution.

The first step towards long-term growth is creating evergreen content that remains relevant and valuable over time. This type of content can continually attract new viewers and retain existing ones, contributing to a steady increase in channel visibility and subscriber base. Evergreen content should be complemented with timely pieces that tap into current trends or events, balancing immediate viewer interest with long-term value.

Another crucial aspect is diversification. Creators should explore various content formats, such as live streams, tutorials, vlogs, or interviews, to cater to different viewer preferences and occasions. Diversification extends beyond content types; it also means expanding presence across multiple platforms to mitigate risks associated with algorithm changes or platform-specific issues. Building an ecosystem around your brand ensures stability and opens up additional revenue streams through merchandise sales, sponsorships, or exclusive content on other platforms.

- Investing in community building is essential for sustained growth. Engaging with your audience through comments, social media interactions, and community posts creates a loyal fanbase more likely to support your endeavors long term.

- Data analytics play a pivotal role in planning for growth. Regularly analyzing performance metrics helps creators understand what works best for their audience, allowing them to refine their content strategy accordingly.

- Collaboration with other creators can introduce your channel to new audiences while fostering a sense of community within the platform's ecosystem.

In conclusion, planning for long-term growth on digital platforms requires a multifaceted approach that emphasizes quality content creation, audience engagement, brand diversification, and data-driven strategies. By staying adaptable yet consistent in their efforts, creators can build a sustainable presence that thrives amidst the ever-changing digital landscape.

References:

- Derral Eves. "The YouTube Formula: How Anyone Can Unlock the Algorithm to Drive Views, Build an Audience, and Grow Revenue." This book provides insights into understanding and leveraging YouTube's algorithm for growth.

- Roberto Blake. "YouTube Channel Checklist: Ideas for Creating Valuable Content." An online resource offering strategies for content creation and channel optimization.

- Tim Schmoyer. "30 Days to a Better YouTube Channel." A course designed to improve channel performance through daily actionable steps focusing on audience engagement and content value.

- Sunny Lenarduzzi. "How to Grow Your YouTube Channel in 2023." An online guide that covers various aspects of building a successful YouTube presence, including content strategy and audience interaction.

"How To Grow On YouTube As An Adult" serves as an essential guide for mature individuals looking to make their mark on the YouTube platform. This non-fiction book addresses the unique challenges faced by adults entering the digital content creation space, offering tailored advice for those seeking to share their passions, transition careers, or generate additional income through YouTube. The significance of this book lies in its focus on adult creators, a group often overlooked in discussions about digital creativity and social media success.

The book covers a range of critical topics necessary for building a successful YouTube channel. It begins with strategies for identifying one's niche, emphasizing the importance of finding a balance between personal interests and market demand. This section includes practical exercises for refining focus and methods for validating niche choices. Following this, it offers content creation tips designed to fit into the busy schedules of adults juggling multiple responsibilities. Readers will learn efficient planning, filming, and editing techniques alongside time management strategies.

Another key area explored is SEO optimization, where the author demystifies YouTube's algorithm and provides accessible techniques for making videos more discoverable. The book also delves into monetization strategies beyond traditional ad revenue, covering sponsorships, merchandise sales, and membership platforms while offering advice on negotiating deals without compromising content integrity.

Building a community around one's channel is highlighted as crucial for growth and viewer loyalty. The book suggests effective communication techniques for engaging with audiences and fostering positive interactions. Lastly, it tackles common challenges such as dealing with criticism, managing privacy concerns, and staying motivated during slow growth periods.

In summary, "How To Grow On YouTube As An Adult" is an empowering resource that equips adult YouTubers with the knowledge to navigate the complexities of YouTube growth successfully. It stands out by providing practical advice grounded in real-world experience, focusing on personal development alongside platform growth.

www.ingramcontent.com/pod-product-compliance
Lightning Source LLC
Chambersburg PA
CBHW050111230526
45470CB00004B/1778